C000216817

A Visit
From Miss Prothero
(*from* Office Suite)

A Play

Alan Bennett

Samuel French – London
New York – Sydney – Toronto – Hollywood

A VISIT FROM MISS PROTHERO

First transmitted by the BBC on 11th January, 1978, with the following cast of characters:

Mr Dodsworth   Hugh Lloyd
Miss Prothero   Patricia Routledge

Directed by Stephen Frears

The action takes place in the living-room of Mr Dodsworth's semi-detached house

Time—the present

COPYRIGHT INFORMATION
(See also page ii)

A VISIT FROM MISS PROTHERO

The living-room of a semi-detached house. A worn, comfortable, cosy place

There are two doors: one to the hall, the other to the kitchen

Dozing in an armchair and similarly worn, cosy and comfortable is Mr Dodsworth, a man in his sixties. In a cardigan and carpet slippers with the top button of his trousers undone Mr Dodsworth is retired. He is just having five minutes and, unless one counts the budgie, he is alone

A few moments pass, sufficient for the tranquillity of the household to be established, then the door-chimes go

Mr Dodsworth does not respond

The chimes go again

Mr Dodsworth stirs and, fastening the top button of his trousers, gets up

Mr Dodsworth (*addressing the budgie*) Who's this then, Millie? Who's this?

He goes out, leaving the living-room door open. The front door opens

(*Off*) Is it you, Miss Prothero?
Miss Prothero (*off*) It is.
Mr Dodsworth (*off*) I didn't expect to see you.

While Mr Dodsworth hovers in the living-room doorway the visitor comes in boldly. It is a middle-aged woman, who runs a critical eye over the warm, comfortable, cosy room. She is none of these things

Miss Prothero I was beginning to think I'd got the wrong house.
Mr Dodsworth Why? Had you been stood there long?
Miss Prothero A minute or two.
Mr Dodsworth No, it's the right house. Number 59. The Dodsworth residence.

Miss Prothero I rang twice.

Mr Dodsworth To tell you the truth I was just having five minutes.

Miss Prothero I'm surprised. You were the one who couldn't abide a nap.

Mr Dodsworth Was I? You'll take your coat off?

Miss Prothero I was waiting to be asked.

He starts to help her off with her coat

I shan't stop.

Mr Dodsworth No, but . . .

Miss Prothero I still have my back, so I'll keep my undercoat on.

Mr Dodsworth is tugging at her cardigan sleeve, trying to take it off

That's my undercoat.

Mr Dodsworth Sorry. Sorry.

Miss Prothero This time of year can be very treacherous. (*Spring, summer, autumn, winter . . . to Miss Prothero the seasons were all potential assassins*) And I'd best keep my hat on as well. I don't want another sinus do.

Mr Dodsworth is about to bear away the fainted form of Miss Prothero's swagger coat when she stops him

I'm forgetting my hanky. (*She takes it out of the pocket and blows her nose*)

Mr Dodsworth carries her coat out to the hallstand

There's half a dozen people I ought to go see, only I thought you might be feeling a bit out of it. I said to Doreen, "I know Mr Dodsworth, he'll be wanting to be brought up to date."

Mr Dodsworth (*off*) What on?

Miss Prothero What on? Work! Warburtons!

Mr Dodsworth (*off*) Oh, *work*. No. No.

Miss Prothero (*to herself*) I'm sorry I came then. (*She remains standing in one spot, surveying the room*)

Mr Dodsworth bustles back

Mr Dodsworth What I mean, of course, is I do want to be brought up to date but to tell you the truth, Peggy, since I've left I've hardly had time to turn round. What with bowling on Tuesdays and my Rotary thing on Fridays and Gillian and the kiddies bobbing in every five minutes, I honestly haven't given work a thought. Which is amazing when you think I was there all those years. But you know what they say: retirement, it's a full-time job. Ha ha.

Miss Prothero doesn't laugh. She vaguely flinches. Miss Prothero is one of those people who only see jokes by appointment

What about you? Have you taken the day off?

Miss Prothero Mr Dodsworth, when did I take a day off? In all the years we worked together when did I ever take a day off? Even the day I buried mother I came in in the afternoon to do the backlog. It shows you how out of touch you are. What day is it?

Mr Dodsworth Thursday.

Miss Prothero What week? Week 35. The Works Outing.

Mr Dodsworth Are we into week 35? There you are. It just shows you how I've lost track. You've not gone then?

Miss Prothero After last year? I haven't.

Mr Dodsworth Is it Bridlington again?

Miss Prothero Langdale Pikes.

Mr Dodsworth A beauty spot! That's a departure. It's generally always Bridlington. Or thereabouts. Langdale Pikes. Quite scenic.

Miss Prothero That's because Design put their spoke in. Costing and Estimates pulled a long face but it's only fair: it goes by departments. I dread to think where they'll choose next year.

Mr Dodsworth Whose turn is it then?

Miss Prothero (*ominously*) Maintenance and Equipment. Mind you, as I said to Mr Butterfield in Projects, with a coachload of animals the venue is immaterial.

Mr Dodsworth It's only once a year.

Miss Prothero That coach, if it stopped once it stopped several times. Mr Teasdale's never looked me in the eye since. Wendy Walsh won't even speak to him.

Mr Dodsworth I never thought he had it in him.

Miss Prothero He was a wild beast. It's Mrs Teasdale I feel sorry for. Married to him. And she only has one kidney. Anyway, Mr Skinner soon sized him up. He kept filling out 5D forms the whole of the first week: that took the wind out of his sails. I thought, "Full marks to Mr Skinner."

Mr Dodsworth Oh yes, Skinner. How is Skinner?

Miss Prothero Getting into his stride. I think he'll turn out to be a bit of a dynamo.

Mr Dodsworth He seemed a nice fellow. Young, but nice. Aren't you going to sit down?

Miss Prothero I was waiting to be asked. (*She settles herself in a chair by the fire*) No. Don't you worry about Mr Skinner.

Mr Dodsworth I wasn't.

Miss Prothero He wouldn't thank you if you did. He goes his own way does Mr Skinner. Our new broom! All I wonder is how someone of his calibre bothers wasting his time at Warburtons. He could go anywhere, Mr Skinner. Brazil. New York. They'd snap him up. (*She points to a wedding photograph on a table by where she is sitting*) Is that Mrs Dodsworth?

Mr Dodsworth Which?

Miss Prothero This woman with her arm through yours.

Mr Dodsworth We'd just got married.

Miss Prothero Oh. I suppose that's why she's smiling. Funny dress.

Mr Dodsworth Is it? They're coming back now.

Miss Prothero Like that? Are they? I haven't seen them. No, I was saying, it's not that I'm short of somewhere to go. I've got one or two people who're always begging me to pop in, one of them a retired chiropodist, but I knew you'd be wanting all the latest gen from Warburtons. I'd have come sooner but it's been a busy time, as you can imagine.

Mr Dodsworth What with?

Miss Prothero With the change-over. The new regime. I just bobbed on a bus. With the 23 going right up Gelderd Road it makes it very handy. You can tell; I was coming out of the house at twenty-five to and it's only ten past now.

Mr Dodsworth You must have been lucky.

Miss Prothero It's just a matter of pitching it right. Don't think I've ever had to wait for a bus, ever.

Mr Dodsworth I've started pottery classes.

Miss Prothero Whatever for?

Mr Dodsworth (*indicating an ashtray on the table*) I made this last week.

Miss Prothero Oh. What is it?

Mr Dodsworth It's an ashtray.

Miss Prothero I didn't think you smoked. You wouldn't recognize the office now. There's all sorts been happening.

Mr Dodsworth There has to me. I'm starting cooking classes.

Miss Prothero Cookery? For men?

Mr Dodsworth For anybody. There's several of us retired people, it's a right nice young lady does the teaching. It's cordon bleu.

Miss Prothero Cordon bleu!

Mr Dodsworth I thought it was about time I branched out a bit.

Miss Prothero I can see I've come to the wrong place. I thought you'd be busting for news of Warburtons and here you are all set up with pottery and cookery, out and about every night. We must seem very dull.

Mr Dodsworth No, Peggy, you're wrong. You don't. But the way I look at it is this: I spent half my life at Warburtons and apart from Winnie it was my whole world. I've been retired four months and I'm beginning to see it's *not* the whole world, not by a long chalk. I was there thirty years, it's time I branched out.

Miss Prothero Well, there you are, you say it's not the whole world: I got three letters last week from Japan, there was a firm enquiry from Zambia and Mr Skinner says once we get a foothold in these oil-producing countries, there's no reason why the whole of the Middle East shouldn't be banging on the door.

Mr Dodsworth At Warburtons? Really?

Miss Prothero We had a delegation round last week from Rumania.

Mr Dodsworth They'd come a long way.

Miss Prothero Mr Skinner introduced me. Considering they were from behind the Iron Curtain, I found them very charming.

Mr Dodsworth What do they want coming round from Rumania?

Miss Prothero We've got Mr Skinner to thank for that. He's a leading light in the Chamber of Trade. He says Warburtons is part of a much wider world picture. Export or die. And he runs that office with the smoothness of a well-oiled machine. Not that I'm saying you didn't.

Mr Dodsworth Well, it was friendly.

Miss Prothero Yes. He's put a stop to all that.

Mr Dodsworth What?

Miss Prothero All that going to the toilet. Mr Teasdale falling out for a smoke. Pauline Lucas coming down for half an hour at a stretch. He soon had her taped.

Mr Dodsworth Is she still ginger?

Miss Prothero Who?

Mr Dodsworth Pauline. She was blonde. I thought ginger suited her better.

Miss Prothero I thought it was a bit on the common side. And there's not so much of the Pauline nowadays, either. People get called by their proper titles. It's Miss Prothero, Mrs Lucas. None of this Pauline and Peggying. Status. I like it. (*Suddenly she lunges for the electric fire*) Could we have a bar off? Miss Cardwell's had her baby.

Mr Dodsworth Who?

Miss Prothero Miss Cardwell. In the typing pool.

Mr Dodsworth Maureen? Had a baby? I thought she had rheumatic fever. In Nottingham.

Miss Prothero Well if she did she got it knitting bootees.

Mr Dodsworth Boy?

Miss Prothero Girl. The image of him, so I'm told.

Mr Dodsworth Who?

Miss Prothero Mr Corkery.

Mr Dodsworth In despatch?

Miss Prothero Costing. He's been transferred.

Mr Dodsworth Poor Maureen.

Miss Prothero Poor nothing. She waltzed down with some snaps of it last week. I didn't know where to put myself.

Mr Dodsworth Will she keep it?

Miss Prothero She'll keep it all right. Same as Christine Thoseby kept hers. Park it in the day nursery all day and come in dressed up to the nines. Equal pay! They don't deserve it. I ran into her the other day, Christine. Yellow cashmere costume, high boots. That's the trouble these days: people don't know where to draw the line. (*Pause*) Food in the canteen doesn't get any better, mince three times last week. Somebody's making something on the side, meals that price. You never see that supervisor but what she's got a parcel. Wicked. If I were the fifth floor that's where I'd clamp down.

Mr Dodsworth They always seem to have a smile, that's the main thing.

Miss Prothero Of course they have a smile. Something to smile about, the money they make. That supervisor's just gone and got herself a little bungalow at Roundhay.

Mr Dodsworth doesn't want to know about the canteen, mince on the menu or the supervisor's bungalow at Roundhay. He doesn't want to know about Warburtons at all. There were worlds elsewhere

Mr Dodsworth (*going over to the birdcage*) You haven't met Millie, have you? (*To the budgie*) This is Miss Prothero. Say how do you do.

Millie doesn't oblige

She's been a bit depressed today.

Miss Prothero (*not to be turned aside by the state of mind of an unknown budgie*) I wasn't aware they got depressed. What've they got to be depressed about? They don't have to work for a living. (*Pause*) I've changed my extension.

Mr Dodsworth Oh yes?

Miss Prothero You remember I used to be 216. Now I'm 314.

Mr Dodsworth Going up in the world.

Miss Prothero Doreen Glazier's 216 now. Big change for her. Preston and Fosters rang last week and didn't realize. I saw Mr Skinner smile. She's still got that nasty eczema.

Mr Dodsworth Doreen? Poor girl.

Miss Prothero The doctor thinks it's nerves. I think it's those tights. Man-made fibres don't do for everybody: I pay if I wear crimplene. But Doreen's never really been happy since her transfer. I ran into Miss Brunskill in the lift and she says when Doreen was in Credit and Settlement she was a different person. How old do you think she is now?

Mr Dodsworth Doreen?

Miss Prothero Miss Brunskill.

Mr Dodsworth Fifty?

Miss Prothero Forty-eight, I was surprised. I saw it on her 253. I thought she was nearer sixty. That's with being on the fifth floor. It takes it out of you.

Mr Dodsworth (*restive and bored*) Could you drink a cup of tea?

Miss Prothero Tea? With my kidneys?

Mr Dodsworth I forgot.

Miss Prothero I wish I could forget. Tea—you might as well offer me hydrochloric acid.

Mr Dodsworth Well, coffee?

Miss Prothero Only if it's very weak.

Mr Dodsworth gets up and starts to exit

How are your waterworks?

Mr Dodsworth Sorry?

Miss Prothero You were having a spot of trouble with your waterworks, don't you remember?

Mr Dodsworth They're champion now, thanks very much.

Mr Dodsworth thankfully leaves the room to put the kettle on

Miss Prothero bides her time

Miss Prothero (*calling*) And do you still have your appliance?

There is no answer

Is it still playing you up?

Mr Dodsworth (*off*) I never think about it now.

Miss Prothero (*still calling*) Typical of this country. Can't even make a (*she says the dreadful word with a kind of triumph*) truss.

Mr Dodsworth (*off*) Sugar?

Miss Prothero If there is any.

Mr Dodsworth returns

Mr Dodsworth We're just waiting the kettle.

Miss Prothero In which case, if you don't mind, I think I'll pay a call.

Mr Dodsworth It's up on the landing. Facing you as you go up.

Miss Prothero exits

He listens as she goes upstairs, opens the door of the toilet and bolts it after her

Then get off home you bad, boring bitch. (*He goes over to the birdcage*) What does she want to come on round here for in the first place? We're quite happy, aren't we Millie? Aren't we? We're quite happy. (*He gets out from the sideboard a little table and two plates as the toilet is flushed*)

Miss Prothero returns as:

(*He starts to go out to the kitchen; cryptically*) Kettle.

Mr Dodsworth exits

Miss Prothero (*looking critically at the mantelpiece*) Is this your clock?

Mr Dodsworth (*off*) Yes. It's a nice one, don't you think?

Miss Prothero shouts some of the following to the kitchen. Other remarks she makes to herself

Miss Prothero Quite honestly I was against that. I spoke up when it was first mooted. Well I felt I had to. Time to give someone a clock is at the start of his career not the end. I said anyway. What do you want to know the time for, sat here? Time dribbling away and nothing to look forward to. Tick-tock tick-tock. It would get on my nerves.

Mr Dodsworth (*off*) It's not got a tick. It's electric.

Miss Prothero You've still got the hands going round. It saves winding, I suppose.

Mr Dodsworth returns with a tray, two cups and some cake

Mr Dodsworth There's more to a clock than time. It's a memento. It makes me think back.

Miss Prothero You were saying just now you didn't want to think back.

Mr Dodsworth Well I do and I don't. You know how it is.

Miss Prothero My proposal was something useful. An electric blanket.

Mr Dodsworth Yes, only I like the inscription. You couldn't inscribe a blanket.

Miss Prothero You were lucky it wasn't a rose-bowl. Another useless article.

Mr Dodsworth Cake? It's our Gillian's.

Miss Prothero (*in her eyes this is no recommendation*) Just a small piece. No. Half that.

Mr Dodsworth Winnie and I were given a canteen of cutlery when we were first married. It's stood us in good stead (*He displays the canteen of cutlery*) See. Cake knives, everything. (*He selects her a cake knife*)

Miss Prothero I can manage. They're only to wash up. (*She drinks her coffee like medicine, every swallow loud, cavernous and unignorable*)

Mr Dodsworth flees to the sideboard, then to the birdcage

What was Millie like?

Mr Dodsworth Millie?

Miss Prothero Millie. Mrs Dodsworth.

Mr Dodsworth *Winnie*. Millie's the budgie.

Miss Prothero I mean Winnie. (*Pause*) What was she like?

Mr Dodsworth Well ... very nice. She was very nice. She was a saint. A real saint. (*Pause*) Pretty. When she was younger. Full of life. Not very practical.

Miss Prothero Women aren't.

Mr Dodsworth Though she rigged this place out. There was nothing here, nothing. She did all this herself, curtains and covers. She could make a place cosy, could Winnie. She used to read a lot. Read all sorts. Naomi Jacob. Leo Walmsley. Phyllis Bentley. The Brontës. She'd read them all.

Miss Prothero I suppose it's very nice if you've got the time. Me, I never open a book from one year's end to the next. Anyway, it's all escape.

Mr Dodsworth I don't know it was with Win.

Miss Prothero Oh yes, travel, romance. The mind's elsewhere. She'd be a bit lonely here all day, you at Warburtons. She never went out to work?

Mr Dodsworth Well, she'd got our Gillian to look after. But she did all sorts. Rugs, crochet. These mats are hers. She never saw the clock. I'd have liked her to see the clock. What about your family?

Miss Prothero My what?

Mr Dodsworth Family.

Miss Prothero Do you mean Father?

Mr Dodsworth Oh yes. I'm sorry. Your mother died.

Miss Prothero She didn't die. Father killed her.

Mr Dodsworth Oh?

This is not the response Miss Prothero is after. Pause

That's news to me.

Miss Prothero Over forty-two years of marriage, slowly, day by day, inch by inch, smiling and smiling in the sight of the whole world, gently and politely with every appearance of kindness, he killed her.

There is an endless pause

Mr Dodsworth What did he do for a living?
Miss Prothero He was a gents' outfitter.
Mr Dodsworth Really?
Miss Prothero It was Other Women.
Mr Dodsworth Oh ay.
Miss Prothero In droves.

What lives other people led. A gents' outfitter in Leeds with droves of Other Women. And he had hardly lived at all, thought Dodsworth

Mr Dodsworth What was he like?
Miss Prothero Tall. Little tash. A limp.
Mr Dodsworth A limp?
Miss Prothero Mother always said that helped. They felt safe.

Women have always felt safe with me, thinks Mr Dodsworth. But then they were. Miss Prothero obviously feels quite safe. But then she is

Mr Dodsworth Is he still living?
Miss Prothero Oh yes. He's had a stroke. He's in a home at Farnley. Paralysed all down one side. They have to do everything for him. Sits and sits and sits.
Mr Dodsworth Still. He has his memories.

Yes, Miss Prothero thinks, of Other Women

Miss Prothero Once he got taken for Ronald Colman.
Mr Dodsworth Who?
Miss Prothero Father.
Mr Dodsworth Did Ronald Colman limp?
Miss Prothero No, but he had a tash.

Mr Dodsworth thinks of old Mr Prothero, paralysed all down one side up at Farnley, sat with his memories of droves of Other Women and once having been taken for Ronald Colman

Mr Dodsworth It doesn't paralyse the memory, then, a stroke?
Miss Prothero Why?
Mr Dodsworth It leaves you with half your movements. I wondered whether it left you with half your memories.
Miss Prothero Well you wouldn't know, would you? If you can't remember it, how do you know you've forgotten it?

*Mr Dodsworth tries to bend his mind round this, fails and falls back
on Art*

Mr Dodsworth Do you fancy a bit of music?

Miss Prothero I don't mind.

Mr Dodsworth Do you not like music?

Miss Prothero I don't mind. If it's played I listen to it.

Mr Dodsworth That's something else I might take up. Musical
appreciation. They have classes in that.

Miss Prothero I don't care for the violin. Not on its own.

Mr Dodsworth I think you'll like this. I do. (*He puts a cassette in
the player*)

It is the theme from Un Homme et Une Femme. *It goes on and on
and on. Miss Prothero sits awkwardly waiting while Mr Dodsworth
listens appreciatively. She gives it a minute or two before deciding
it's time to break the spell, which she does by suddenly getting to her
feet*

Miss Prothero They've introduced music in the lifts now. That
was Mr Skinner's suggestion. It's industrial psychology. Is that
clock fast?

Mr Dodsworth No.

Miss Prothero I was thinking of catching the twenty past.

Mr Dodsworth Oh yes. (*He turns off the music*)

Miss Prothero But I've a bit yet. (*She sits down again. Pause*) I like
to get back before dark. Two women attacked on the 73 last
week. You'd never get me upstairs. It's just asking for it. (*Pause*)
I don't seem to have told you much news. Mind you, if I told
you everything that had been going on I don't suppose you'd
thank me.

Mr Dodsworth Well you have. You've brought me up to date on
Maureen's baby. Doreen's skin trouble. It's just put me in the
picture a bit. It's all I want.

Miss Prothero That's only the half of it.

Mr Dodsworth Perhaps, Peggy. But you see, it's this way. I was
with Warburtons thirty years. Thirty years that saw big changes,
some, I flatter myself, the work of yours truly. And doubtless
the next thirty years will be the same. More changes. Except
now it's somebody else's turn. It's time for me to stand aside and
let them get on with it. I don't resent that, Peggy. A chapter is
closed. A new one begins. The wheel turns. You see, when you

get to my age, you accept that, Peggy. I'm not saying I didn't make my mark. I did. In my own way I revolutionized Warburtons. Incidentally, that reminds me. I've got something I want you to take.

Mr Dodsworth goes out into the hall and can be heard rummaging under the stairs

(*Off*) When I left I told Mr Skinner I'd let him have this, when I can find it. You can take it him, if you don't mind. Here we are.

He comes in with a large, flat parcel wrapped in worn brown paper and tied with string. He tears off the brown paper. It is very dusty

Recognize it?

It is a framed chart of inter-office procedure, chains of authority, Central, District, Sub-District, and so on, drawn up in an elaborate and decorative way, in various colours. It may be more convenient to have it on a roll of paper, rather than in a frame

Miss Prothero I recognize it of course. It's the old revised lay-out.
Mr Dodsworth It's basically the same as the one we have in the office but old Mr Trowbridge in Design ... except it wasn't called Design then, in the Drawing Shop ... I got him to make me a bit fancier one for Winnie really. She used to hear me talking about the lay-out that much, I had it done for her. It's a nice thing, I thought it'd go well in Mr Skinner's office. Mind it's a bit mucky. I'll get a cloth.

Mr Dodsworth exits to the kitchen

Miss Prothero Well! This brings back memories! (*It may only be because the diagram is dirty but Miss Prothero is looking at it with some disdain*)

Mr Dodsworth returns with a cloth and cleans it up, whereupon:

Miss Prothero condescends to look closer and even seems interested

Mr Dodsworth It's only the names that are different ... and there's the three new departments but basically it's the same set-up as we've got today. Fancy. (*He points to the date*) 1947! It was cold. Bitter cold. We used to be starved stiff. Everybody in Credit and Settlement used to be sat there in their overcoats.

Miss Prothero I remember. The place must have been a shambles then.

Mr Dodsworth It was, Peggy. It was.

Miss Prothero No system at all.

Mr Dodsworth How could there be a system when filing was on three floors. You'd be running up and down those stairs all afternoon looking for a voucher and then find it was over at Dickinson Road all the time. It beats me how we ever got any payments in at all in them days.

Miss Prothero It was old Mr Warburton's fault. Nobody could do anything with him stuck there.

Mr Dodsworth If you've built a firm up from being one room then naturally you think you know best.

Miss Prothero He was the only one who knew where anything was. You should delegate. He couldn't delegate.

Mr Dodsworth By but he was a worker! There till ten every night.

Miss Prothero But there was no system. System is what you want. It was all hand to mouth.

Mr Dodsworth I tell you, Peggy ...

There is no need to tell Peggy anything. She is sitting there, smiling a distant smile because she knows it all and a great deal more besides

... when I first took over in Credit and Settlement I did nothing at all for about a month. I just sat there in that office in my overcoat trying to fathom it all out. How it functioned. How it should function. How it could be made to function. And eventually I thought, "Well, Arthur, if you can only get the filing on to a proper footing that'll be a start." I reckoned that'd maybe take two or three months at the outside. Do you know how long it took? Four years. But I reckon that four years saved Warburtons thousands, hundreds of thousands in the end. Because out of it came ... (*he refers to all this on the diagram*) direct debiting, inter-departmental docketing, direct directorial access, the marrying of receipts and invoices and really, all the lay-out of the new complex. It's all here. In embryo. Do you know what the turn-round was when I first came into that office?

Miss Prothero Ten days.

Mr Dodsworth Three weeks. And you know what it was when I left? Well, you know what it was when I left. Forty-eight hours.

And there it is. All I like to think is that when the fifth floor rings up for a 237 and it's there in five minutes there'll be somebody thinking—"Thank you, Arthur Dodsworth." Anyway, you take it. Give it Mr Skinner with my compliments. I'm not wanting to rush you off but you don't want to miss your bus. I'll put you some clean paper round it. (*He rummages in a drawer*)

Miss Prothero The trouble is Mr Skinner's very particular about anything on the walls. He had Doreen take down all her postcards. And Mr Teasdale's silly notices. "You don't have to be mad to work here but it helps." I never thought that was funny. Mr Skinner didn't either. Now the walls are confined to relevant information.

Mr Dodsworth This is relevant information, right enough. The basics are the same as they are today. I took him through it before I left. He soon had the hang of it. Of course that's the beauty of it. Logic and simplicity.

He exits to the hall and returns with Miss Prothero's coat

Still if you don't want to take it, I'll pop by with it sometime.

Miss Prothero I should hang on to it. It'll be like your clock. A memento.

Mr Dodsworth Peggy. This is a working diagram.

Miss Prothero Things have changed.

Mr Dodsworth Not basically. Basically things are the same. (*He stops and looks at her*) Aren't they?

Miss Prothero That's what I've been trying to say. Only you would go on about all the things you were doing, wider worlds than Warburtons.

Mr Dodsworth What things?

Miss Prothero Cookery classes, pottery. Cordon bleu.

Mr Dodsworth What things?

Miss Prothero I shall miss my bus.

Mr Dodsworth You won't. That clock's fast.

Miss Prothero Your presentation clock fast? You've not had it six months.

Mr Dodsworth I didn't like to say. The electric's poor here. I think that affects it. You said things have changed. What things?

Miss Prothero sits down heavily

Miss Prothero Everything.

Mr Dodsworth *Everything?*

Miss Prothero You haven't really left me much time. However. When I think the damage was done was that first Monday.

Miss Prothero is determined to catch her bus. She is also determined to tell Mr Dodsworth everything. Speed is of the essence

Mr Dodsworth What first Monday?

Miss Prothero Mr Skinner's ... his first Monday we had a really shocking run of 476s and then to cap it all Costing sent up a couple of 248s ... I mean, I think they were trying it on.

Mr Dodsworth They would be. You don't get a 248 once in six months and two together, I never had that in thirty-odd years.

Miss Prothero Well, that put him wrong side out for a start.

Mr Dodsworth Why didn't he just docket them and get the whole lot carted off to the fifth floor?

Miss Prothero What I said to Doreen Glazier. I think he just didn't want to go running upstairs on his first day. It's understandable, but anyway the upshot was we had to go through the whole rigmarole. Those two 248s took all day.

Mr Dodsworth Costing, they want their backsides kicking.

Miss Prothero The next thing I hear he's been in to see Mr Skidmore.

Mr Dodsworth Mr Skidmore!

Miss Prothero Mr Skidmore. He gives him the green light and do you know what the first thing he does is? Revamps the entire docketing system.

Mr Dodsworth But there was nothing wrong with the docketing system.

Miss Prothero Don't tell *me*. I thought of you, Mr Dodsworth. I thought, well I'm glad Mr Dodsworth isn't here to see this. I ran into Mr Butterfield in Accounts. He knew what was happening.

Mr Dodsworth He would.

Miss Prothero No, I said to him it would break Mr Dodsworth's heart. It would have broken your heart.

Mr Dodsworth That's a funny way of going on. You can't mess about with docketing while you've got receipts and invoices married up.

Miss Prothero Right. A fortnight later they were separated.

Mr Dodsworth But it took me four years to get them together.

Miss Prothero It took him two weeks to get them apart. After that it was a short step to Direct Departmental Debiting.

Mr Dodsworth That would have to be entirely restructured.

Miss Prothero Scrapped.

Mr Dodsworth Scrapped!

Miss Prothero We were knee deep in 5D forms and you know Maintenance are never there when they're wanted: I was actually taking them downstairs and bundling them into the incinerator myself. And of course who should I run into on one of the trips but Mr Sillitoe, who was with me my first year in C and S, do you remember, and he laughed and he said——

Mr Dodsworth But what's happened about filing?

Miss Prothero Oh, did I not tell you that? I thought I'd told you that. Filing was all computerized in September anyway. You see what you have to remember about Mr Skinner is that he was six months at Newport Pagnell. He's got all that at his finger tips.

Mr Dodsworth Well, I don't care what you say, our turn-round was forty-eight hours. You can't get much slicker than that.

Miss Prothero Halved.

Mr Dodsworth Halved?

Miss Prothero Halved. Twenty-four hours now, and Mr Skinner says that's only a stage not a target. He envisages something in the range of twelve hours ... even, you'll laugh at this, even same day turnover.

Mr Dodsworth You'll kill yourselves.

Miss Prothero No. Half-past four and I'm generally just sat there. All done and docketed.

Mr Dodsworth What about that ... inter-departmental docketing?

Miss Prothero Oh, we still do that.

Mr Dodsworth That's something.

Miss Prothero Only it's all in alphabetical order now.

Mr Dodsworth Alphabetical order! What kind of a system is that!

Miss Prothero Listen, I must go.

Mr Dodsworth I don't see it. What happens ... what happens if you get a 318 and a 247 on the same sheet? If you don't have direct departmental debit you've got the whole process to go through on two separate dockets.

Miss Prothero Can't happen. Not under the Skinner system. You see they couldn't be on the same sheet in the first place.

Mr Dodsworth They could be on separate receipt dockets but on the same 348.

Miss Prothero Yes, that happened on Friday. Mr Skinner fed it into the computer and it sorted it out in no time.

Mr Dodsworth I think that's an admission of failure.

Miss Prothero It only takes two minutes.

Mr Dodsworth Computers, what are they? Glorified adding machines.

Miss Prothero Don't let Mr Skinner hear you say that. He says a computer is an instrument of the imagination. He says that with another computer, me and Miss Glazier he could run Credit and Settlement single-handed.

Mr Dodsworth That's Newport Pagnell talking.

Miss Prothero I didn't want to tell you all this but you would drag it out of me.

Mr Dodsworth I just want to get a pencil and paper.

Miss Prothero I must run.

Mr Dodsworth Hang on a sec ... (*He starts making calculations*)

Miss Prothero It's a waste of time. You won't crack it. We've been going now for nearly four months and, as I say, Mr Skinner runs that office with the smoothness of a well-oiled machine.

Mr Dodsworth You could catch the ten to, not the twenty past.

Miss Prothero I've my supper to get.

Mr Dodsworth You could have your supper here.

Miss Prothero It's getting dark. Still I can call again. I thought you'd be lonely. I said to Doreen. I bet he's lonely. And it's made a nice little outing. You get out of touch.

Mr Dodsworth It's true. I'd not realized.

Miss Prothero Tell you what I can do. If I come again——

Mr Dodsworth No, you must come.

Miss Prothero —and that's fetch you some copies of the 114s. Glenda'll run more off one or two if I ask her nicely and then you'll be able to see how the procedure works, and that'll set your mind at rest.

Mr Dodsworth Would you do that? That *is* good of you. Oh, Peggy, I should be ever so grateful ...

Miss Prothero Well, we always had a soft spot for one another you and me, didn't we? (*She mouths "bye-bye" silently*)

Miss Prothero exits and Mr Dodsworth follows her into the hall

Mr Dodsworth (*off*) And think on, call round any time. I shall be here. I won't go out. I'll make a point of not going out. Thank you ever so much for coming. Take care.

The front door closes. There is a pause

Mr Dodsworth comes slowly back into the room. He closes the door and picks up the chart, looks at it for a moment or two, then puts it down. He goes over to the birdcage, but without speaking to the bird

Mr Dodsworth stands in his sitting-room feeling his whole life has been burgled, the contents of the years ransacked and strewn about the room. Some items he knows have gone and as the days pass he will remember others. Next time Miss Prothero will tell him more; and he will have less. He sits down in his chair

Oh, Winnie, Winnie.

CURTAIN

FURNITURE AND PROPERTY LIST

On stage: Armchair
              Sideboard. *In it:* canteen of cutlery, small table, two plates
              Table. *On it:* pottery ashtray, wedding photograph
              Chair
              Electric fire
              Birdcage with budgerigar
              Clock
              Cassette-player
              Cassettes

Off stage: Tray with two cups and cake **(Mr Dodsworth)**
              Chart **(Mr Dodsworth)**
              Cloth **(Mr Dodsworth)**

LIGHTING PLOT

Practical fittings required: electric fire

Interior. A sitting-room. The same throughout

To open: Full general lighting,
electric fire glow

EFFECTS PLOT

Cue 1 When ready   (Page 1)
Doorbell rings. Then rings again

Cue 2 **Miss Prothero** exits   (Page 8)
Sound of steps going upstairs; door opens and closes

Cue 3 **Mr Dodsworth:** "We're quite happy."   (Page 8)
Toilet flushes

Cue 4 **Mr Dodsworth:** puts a cassette in player (Page 12)
Theme from "Un Homme et Une Femme" plays*

Cue 5 **Mr Dodsworth:** turns off the music (Page 12)
Cut music

Cue 6 **Mr Dodsworth** goes out into the hall (Page 13)
Sound of rummaging from hall

MADE AND PRINTED IN GREAT BRITAIN BY
LATIMER TREND & COMPANY LTD PLYMOUTH

MADE IN ENGLAND